Occasional Paper

4

I0019066

Demystifying Chinese Cyber Sovereignty

Ranjani Srinivasan

KNOWLEDGE WORLD

KW Publishers Pvt Ltd
New Delhi

The Chennai Centre for China Studies (C3S), registered under the Tamil Nadu Societies Registration Act 1975 (83/2008 dated 4th April 2008), is a non-profit public policy think tank with the following objectives.

- Carry out in-depth studies of developments relating to China with priority to issues of interest to India such as
  1. Geopolitical, economic and strategic dynamics of India-China relations.
  2. China's internal dynamics.
  3. The Sino-Indian border issue.
  4. China's relations with South Asian countries.
  5. Prospects of Sino-Indian economic and trade relations.
  6. Future evolution of China's politics and its impact on India and the world.
  7. China - India - ASEAN relations.
  8. China's emerging role in SAARC.
  9. Growing importance of South India for Chinese interaction and economic investment.
  10. India - China - Southeast Asia cultural links.
- Suggest viable solutions/policy alternatives on the basis of studies to the strategic planners and decision makers in India, on issues of bilateral, regional and global importance.
- Create public opinion, particularly in South India, on the implications arising out of China's emergence as a leading global power.
- Provide a forum for dialogue with China scholars in India and abroad and give space for expression of alternate opinions on China-related topics.
- Provide a sound data base for research on China with special attention to tapping information available in Chinese language material, so as to benefit scholars, media and think tanks in India as well as rest of the world.
- Address the requirements of the business community in India, particularly informing them about the nature of emerging business opportunities and problems while dealing with China.
- Liaise with think tanks specialising on China, both in India and abroad, with the objective of exchanging views.
- Organise lecture discussions and seminars on topics of current interest.
- Interact with institutions of higher learning in South India to create awareness about developments in China.
- Bring out publications relating to China - books, edited volumes, monographs and occasional papers.

ISBN   978-93-87324-01-5   Paperback
ISBN   978-93-87324-02-2   ebook

Published in India by Kalpana Shukla

KW Publishers Pvt Ltd
4676/21, First Floor, Ansari Road, Daryaganj, New Delhi 110002
Phone: +91.11.23263498/43528107
Email: kw@kwpub.com • www.kwpub.com

Printed and bound in India.

Contents

Dedicated to
My parents, for teaching me the
value of character.

Acknowledgements

At the outset, I extend my thanks to Ms Asma Masood and Commodore Vasan for giving me the opportunity to gain experience as an intern at the Chennai Centre for China Studies. Their constant guidance, support and feedback have helped me improve the quality of my writing and research. This project would have been incomplete without the inputs of Prof Sonika Gupta, who took great interest in my work. I also thank my senior from college, Madhura Balasubramaniam, who introduced me to the basics of foreign policy writing and has helped with timely inputs and suggestions since day one.

Preface

In today's globalised world, flow of information between nations has never played a more important role. Communication has assumed a significant role as an intricate socio-cultural phenomenon that influences a variety of activities across countries and is tied to the political, economic and technological developments in all countries. In this context, it is interesting to examine how the Chinese Communist Party (CCP) has been taking several measures to regulate the flow of information by controlling the international cyber space as a part of its political agenda.

One of the measures adopted by the Chinese government is the proposal for 'cyber sovereignty'. The Chinese government's call for cyber sovereignty highlights its intention to extend its claim to global power into the territory of Information and Communication Technology (ICT). This has multiple consequences on several realms of significance within and outside the Chinese borders: the intertwining of cyber space with military security, the rise of China as a digital economy and its relationship with member nations of several international bodies are some areas of importance.

China's call for cyber sovereignty does not come without roadblocks. Rigid cyber security regulations present problems in the form of data encryption, theft of intellectual property rights, data localisation and hacking, to name a few. This paper outlines such roadblocks while also examining further challenges and opportunities that the Chinese cyber space holds. Finally, the paper examines the functioning of the American Multi-National Corporation (MNC), Apple, in China in the backdrop of the whip cracking attitude of the Chinese government towards information security and cyber security.

Foreword

China follows a unique path towards the goal of superpower status. The Party has guided the country exceedingly well but exercises extraordinary control on what the population can think and practice. Success achieved is in good measure due to acquisition and assimilation of technological capability. Now China looks to preserve the short-term success while continuing to move forward.

The technology of the future is largely based on Information and Communication Technology (ICT). By its very nature, ICT facilitates rapid and easy flow of ideas across national borders. The Party in China is concerned about inflow of ideas that could upset the current control it has on the population gained through censorship of the Internet.

There is also the desire to deter cyber attacks by others while maintaining a capability for engaging in such actions on others, if and when needed. In effect the goal is to become a digital superpower and be in a position to influence the future of cyber space encompassing Artificial Intelligence, Internet of Things,Quantum Cryptography and other innovations.

These considerations have led China to propose the concept of cyber sovereignty, with total control of all cyber space activities within its borders. Since 2014 China has been organising a World Internet Conference annually with the beguilingly phrased objective of "Internet for openness and shared benefits". There are also attempts to draw in Russia and the other BRICS (Brazil, Russia, India, China, South Africa) countries.

Ranjani presents, in brief, the basic features of China's concept of cyber sovereignty and efforts to promote it. She presents the relevant histories. Hers is a valuable attempt to demystify China's concept for the lay reader.

Mr L.V. Krishnan
Member, C3S
(Former Director, Safety Research Group,
Indira Gandhi Centre for Atomic Research, Kalpakkam)

Demystifying Chinese Cyber Sovereignty

Introduction

The means of measuring a country's power have changed considerably over the last few decades. Power, as it is known today, is no longer measured by a country's military and economic prowess alone, but also by its ability to use technology to convert domestic resources into factors of influence. It is here that the Internet features as a prominent tool for resource-building, research and development, and communication vis-à-vis free exchange of information. Above all, the Internet represents modernity: it is indicative of development and progress in a country. A country is perceived positively by the world when it places fewer restrictions on the use of the Internet by allowing greater access to information. China, which is on the threshold of claiming global power, has much to consider with respect to its restrictive domestic Internet policies.[1]

This paper aims to look beyond China's domestic scenario and analyse its international Internet strategy. The three 'World Internet Conferences' hosted by China between 2014 and 2016 indicate that China is making efforts to provide an international platform for discussing "global cooperation in cyber space governance". During the course of the conferences, President Xi Jinping proposed a cyber space strategy that relies on the concept of "cyber sovereignty". The phrase, in the field of global Internet governance, is used to describe a form of governance which affirms a country's right to decide how its Internet should be managed.[2] This control can be exercised within its own borders, including political, economic and technological activity. Cyber sovereignty, thus, awards a country full control over its Internet infrastructure as well as the content that flows through it. The principle of cyber sovereignty also dictates that surveillance and hacking against any sovereign nation should not be tolerated in cyber space.[3]

Fig 1: Logo of the World Internet Conference, held annually in Wuzhen

Source: Wikipedia (www.https://en.wikipedia.org/wiki/File:WZWIC_logo.png)

The origin of the concept of cyber sovereignty continues to be debated. Some Chinese scholars and officials consider cyber sovereignty a Chinese innovation to further the goals of national security and political sovereignty. They believe that cyber sovereignty reflects China's intentions to become a responsible Internet power. On the other hand, others believe that cyber sovereignty is a product of 'multilateral cooperation' between nations with common goals. Some experts also consider cyber sovereignty to be a product of the Western application of sovereignty to cyber space.[4]

At the outset, the paper seeks to analyse China's understanding of cyber sovereignty and its desire to implement the same. The paper shall begin by gaining an understanding of China's stance on the present Internet governance system before proceeding to outline the relationship between cyber security and cyber sovereignty. It shall then attempt to define some demands made by China in the realm of Information Communication Technology (ICT) that read contrary to China's target of cyber sovereignty. In addition, the paper will provide an outline of how the American MNC, Apple, functions in China and offer an understanding of the barriers to its functioning. The paper shall conclude by examining the impact of cyber sovereignty on some of China's future projects.

Existing Global Internet Order: Who Governs the Internet?
Before delving into the intricacies of China's proposed concept of cyber sovereignty, it is imperative to assess the structure of the existing global Internet. At this juncture, it is important to identify who or what the Internet is governed by. While there is no central 'governing' body, the United States of America has maintained a tight grip on Internet governance since the founding of the Internet. Until recently, the United States Department of Commerce's National Telecommunications and Information Administration (NTIA) had maintained a signed contract with the Internet Corporation for Assigned Names and Numbers (ICANN) to perform the Internet Assigned Numbers Authority (IANA) functions in the interest of the global Internet community.[5]According to ICANN, IANA functions include "the maintenance of the registry of technical Internet protocol parameters; the administration of certain responsibilities associated with Internet DNS root zone and the allocation of Internet numbering resources". In October 2016, the contract between ICANN and NTIA to perform IANA functions officially expired and the United States relinquished its control over Internet governance.[6]

This marked the change of the management and coordination of the Internet's unique identifiers to the private sector. A multi-stakeholder model of governance was adopted. The model sought to include all voices: "...business, academics, technical experts, civil society, governments and many others is the best way to assure that the Internet of tomorrow remains as free, open and accessible as the Internet of today."[7] This historic step is considered to be indicative of full transfer of power from the United States to ICANN, especially with the handing over of the Domain Name System (DNS). This symbolic shift in power marks the end of an era dominated by a unilateral system of Internet governance, and also paves the way for China's multilateral strategy.

China's Preference for Multilateralism in Cyber Space Governance

An alternative to the multi-stakeholder model proposed above is the multilateral model of Internet governance. President Xi, in his statement at the World Internet Conference 2015, indicated China's preference for a form of cyber space governance that features "a multilateral approach with multi-party participation rather than 'one party calling the shots.'"[8] More recently, the *Wuzhen Report on the World Internet Conference* 2016 released in November of the same year presents the recommendations by the High-level Advisory Committee (HAC) regarding the development of Internet governance. The report states:

> Multilateral and multi-parties participation will become the norm for Internet governance. Governments, international organizations, Internet companies, technology communities, civil organizations, academia, and individuals will all take positive actions to safeguard and promote deepening pragmatic cooperation on building the Internet shared and governed by all, and together contribute to its sustainable development.[9]

Multilateralism refers to a system that involves participation from three or more governments or parties. This section aims to understand China's preference for this system, as opposed to the aforementioned multi-stakeholder system, in the context of cyber space governance.

A background paper, published as part of the *World Development Report 2016,* analyses the effectiveness of a multi-stakeholder model for Internet governance. Comparing the multi-stakeholder model with multilateralism, the paper identifies the following differences, as mentioned in the table outlining the 'priorities, aims and goals' of the two systems.[10]

Table 1: 'Priorities, Aims and Goals' as published in Background Paper 'Digital Dividends' as part of the World Development Report 2016

	Characteristics	
Dimensions	Multi-stakeholder	Multilateral/Inter-governmental
Role of Internet	Provide open, secure and global infrastructure for economic and social development and innovation	Protect the (cyber)security of nations and the social and economic development and culture of their citizens
Implications	Stakeholders gain a sense of ownership; keep an open, global and secure Internet; but processes move slowly; and divisive issues can be ignored	Governments gain sense of control; able to act on key concerns of nations, such as security, content controls; but decisions might lag behind technology; issues divisive within nations might block decision-making
Key Objectives to Address	Digital divide or universal access, through investment in ICT infrastructures, services, and capacity building; Millennium Development Goals; avoiding fragmentation, Balkanisation of global Internet; keeping an open Internet	Putting representative and democratic governments in charge of critical Internet resources; more equitable representation of national authorities; maintaining and exerting national sovereignty over cyber security and Internet policy and regulation, such as over expression, privacy and surveillance in ways sensitive to national cultures and interests

As indicated by the column labelled "Multilateral/Inter-governmental", the goals and objectives of a multilateral system of governance involve giving the government full control of discharging critical duties concerning the Internet. The government is also in charge of "maintaining and exerting national sovereignty over cyber security and Internet policy and regulation".[11] These characteristics of the multilateral system are in tandem with China's desire to maintain sovereignty over its cyber space.

Nevertheless, China continues to remain dissatisfied with the present global Internet order. As stated in the *Wuzhen Report on World Internet Development 2016*, "The existing global governance system of basic Internet resources hardly reflects the desires and interests of the majority of countries."[12] It is essential to locate China's lack of satisfaction with the existing order. The answer is multi-pronged and diverse: the cyber realm presents opportunities and challenges on various fronts.

Here, it is important to clarify that China's call for cyber sovereignty cannot be narrowed down to its need to maintain the Chinese domestic Internet system (which is largely censorship-based) alone. China's domestic Internet system continues to function efficiently as China has visibly assumed full control of its cyber space in this domain.

Cyber Sovereignty and Cyber Security: An Important Link in Internet Governance

While it cannot be said that cyber sovereignty is an offshoot of cyber security, it can be said that the two concepts are closely related in the larger scheme of Internet governance. The Chinese notion of cyber security is different from the Western notion. While the West places more importance on technical threats, China's perception of threats is more concerned with ideology. China is more protective of the information going in and out of the country. Information is first sealed off from malware, following which, technical network security is given priority.[13]

President Xi's discourse on cyber sovereignty during the World Internet Conferences largely targeted his Western counterparts for violation of global Internet laws. The driving force behind China's attitude of scepticism towards the global Internet order is its belief that US control of the Internet is undemocratic and perilous for cyber security; China has made repeated calls for eliminating "double standards in cyber security".[14, 15]

The issue of cyber security has, thus, assumed great significance between the US and China, and holds serious potential to affect threat perceptions on either side. Reports of suspected attacks by China on the US in the public and private domains are a common occurrence in the media and the matter has been elevated to a matter of discussion in the Washington DC policy community. China has been named by the US government's 2011 Office of the National Counterintelligence Executive Report as the "most active and persistent" perpetrator of cyber attacks in the United States.[16] The US believes that the cyber attacks present a larger challenge than appears, for a component of these attacks is believed to be organised by the Chinese government.

On the flip side, many spectators believe that more vulnerable than America's systems are those of China. Chinese writers and observers maintain that their systems are more frequently under attack.[17] In 2011, the Ministry of Public Security observed that the number of cyber attacks on Chinese computers had risen by more than 80 percent annually, thereby making China the largest victim of cyber attacks. Chinese writers, thus, respond to such claims by comparing the United States to 'a thief crying stop thief.'[18] The distrust between China and the US in the cyber realm continues to increase each day significantly. Values of importance on either side, such as individual privacy on the US side and concerns of internal stability on the Chinese side, come under further threat.

Countries, apart from the United States, have also reported attacks by China on various occasions. An investigation conducted by researchers in Toronto revealed that a large-scale cyber-espionage ring, known as 'Ghostnet' had penetrated more than 1,200 systems in 103 countries. Victims included foreign embassies, Non-Governmental Organisations (NGOs), news media outlets and international organisations. Tibet-related organisations, including the office of the Dalai Lama, were reported to have come under attack.[19]

Cyber security issues span the political, military and economic narratives. These shall be addressed in the latter half of the paper. This section aims to analyse the problems within the cyber security realm itself, namely: encryption, intellectual property rights, hacking and data localisation.

Encryption

The question of encryption has always played a key role in the interaction between China and other nations on the platform of ICT. A majority of foreign companies that looked to establish themselves in the Chinese market have been hindered by China's harsh encryption policies. Encryption, essentially, is the conversion of data into code so as to secure it and prevent unauthorised access. In 2015, a draft of the Chinese counter-terrorism laws required the "installation of backdoors" and reporting of encryption keys by foreign companies.[20] This was met with disapproval from the United States and the then President, Barack Obama, who claimed that the law "would essentially force all foreign companies, including US companies to turn over to the Chinese government mechanisms whereby they could snoop and keep track of all those services".[21]

Chinese spokespersons have defended themselves in this debate, claiming that both the United States and United Kingdom governments have also requested technology firms to disclose their encryption methods. According to the Chinese government, encryption policies are in compliance with "international common practices".[22]

As a part of its industrial policy in 1999, China banned foreign encryption products and adjudged all commercial encryption standards a state secret. Commercial encryption products could only be produced and sold by the relevant authorities. On further clarification, it was revealed that the law did not seek to impose the ban on products that use encryption as a secondary function (such as laptops, mobile phones, etc.), but only on products whose "core function" was encryption. Nevertheless, the UK and US remain wary of the possibility that the encryption policy could be extended to cover other products as well.[23]

The UK and US have not been unfounded in their suspicions. In 2003, China sought to impose the WLAN (Wireless Local Area Network) Authentication and Privacy Infrastructure (WAPI) as the mandatory standard for any product sold in China. 802.11 Wireless Fidelity (Wi-Fi) was claimed to be banned over "national security concerns", but was believed to have been banned in actuality to reduce payments to foreign patents and encourage domestic producers. More recently, in 2016, when WhatsApp announced their end-to-end encryption policy, China was predicted to launch a Distributed Denial of Service (DDoS) attack on WhatsApp. Contrary to these expectations, WhatsApp continues to function in China, although it is not nearly as popular as its indigenous counterpart, WeChat.[24] WhatsApp, thus, is not expected to pose a tangible threat to the maintenance of control within the Chinese cyber space.

As part of its cyber security initiative, banking reforms have also been fostered in order to increase China's use of domestic technology, in addition to the source code audits and encryption access requirements.[25]

Cyber sovereignty might grant China full and uncontested control over these encryption policies as part of its drive to "protect national Internet space sovereignty" in both domestic and foreign contexts. The vague jurisdiction that is awarded to authorities is likely to be directed towards achieving "security and control in Internet and information core technology, key infrastructure, and important data and information systems", as mentioned by the Chinese legislature in August 2015.[26] These strict policies can be read as an additional fortification of China's drive to control the information flowing in and out of its borders.

Intellectual Property Rights
China continues to have problems concerning its intellectual property rights and its non-compliance with the rules established by the World Trade Organisation.[27] The Office of the US Trade Representative's 2016 Report to Congress on China's WTO Compliance states:

Despite ongoing revisions of laws and regulations relating to intellectual property rights, and greater emphasis on rule of law and enforcement campaigns in China, key weaknesses remain in China's protection and enforcement of intellectual property rights, particularly in the area of trade secret misappropriation. Intellectual property rights holders face not only a complex and uncertain enforcement environment, but also pressure to transfer intellectual property rights to enterprises in China through a number of government policies and practices.[28]

The Unites States has vowed to engage China on issues, including trade secrets, controllable ICT policies, indigenous innovation and controllable ICT policies, among other things. Trademark violations were also cited.[29] According to the aforementioned report, "Of particular and growing concern is the continuing registration of trademarks in bad faith. Although China has taken some steps to address this problem, US companies across industry sectors continue to face Chinese applicants registering their marks and 'holding them for ransom' or seeking to establish a business, building off US companies' global reputations."[30] The report also mentioned that China must remain true to its promise that it shall not advance policies that require the transfer of intellectual property rights as a prerequisite for doing business in China. According to another report released by the American Department of Defence in 2015, titled *The DoD Cyber Strategy*, "China steals Intellectual Property (IP) from global businesses to benefit Chinese companies and undercut US competitiveness."[31]

As Chinese markets continue to expand and draw more companies each day, this discussion becomes more relevant when considering the concept of cyber sovereignty. China is more likely to assume greater control of Intellectual Property Rights (IPR) and associated data flowing within its borders.

Some solutions proposed towards safeguarding technology in China include:

1. Setting up a wholly owned foreign company in China, as opposed to entering a joint venture.

2. Breaking up the manufacturing process to prevent a large group of employees from learning the details of the whole process.
3. Manufacturing more components in-house, instead of out-sourcing them.[32]

The solutions proposed above are not exhaustive. The US, however, has promised to continue its efforts to recommend further steps to be taken by China to address their concerns. Further, China will continue to face the problem of competitiveness in ICT from various countries, and it remains to be seen how China can equal the standards set by international corporations without resorting to theft or sabotage of property rights.

Data Localisation

In another attempt to reinforce its sovereignty, China introduced a new cyber security law which came into effect in June 2017. A part of the law sought to impose rules and regulations on the data flowing in and out of the mainland. According to Article 37 of the law, "Personal information and other important data gathered or produced by critical information infrastructure operators during operations within the mainland territory of the People's Republic of China, shall store it within mainland China."[33]

The government is yet to define what "other important data" means and what falls under Critical Information Infrastructure (CII) guidelines. Earlier reports and documents such as the *Guidelines for Cross-Border Transfer Security Agreement* and the *National Security Law* define important data as that which can "influence or harm the government, state, military, economy, culture, society, technology, information...and other national security matters."[34]

Measures on Security Assessment of Cross-border Transfer of Personal Information and Important Data, which also came into effect in June 2017, states that all "network operators" will be subjected to an assessment of data transfer.[35] The term 'network operators' provides minimal clarity about who owns and manages a network. A number of e-commerce companies are likely to fall within the purview of this term and are likely to be deemed 'critical infrastructure', especially companies such as Alibaba and Tencent, given the personal data held by these companies.[36]

Officials have voiced thoughts about the need to balance national security measures with the global commerce. The Director General of the Cyberspace Administration of China (CAC), Zhao Zeliang, in a meeting in 2017, stated that the government does not seek to hinder globalisation or put a stop to cross-border flow of data as part of the One Belt One Road (OBOR) strategy. The Director General clarified the government's intentions, stating that their purpose was to gain insight into risks that companies may have to take.[37]

Foreign companies now face a number of security measures and reviews, ranging from encryption to data localisation. These measures do not imply that it will henceforth be impossible for foreign companies to do business in China. However, China has much to rethink about as the domestic companies look to go global and expand. Similarly, the US should push for the smooth flow of business-related data across borders when responding to their Chinese counterparts.

More recently, in August 2017, the CAC announced its decision to investigate Tencent's WeChat, Sina's Weibo and Baidu's Tiebu — China's top three Internet giants for potentially violating the cyber security law. These companies have been accused of disobeying China's cyber security law on account of failing to handle the "illegal information uploaded by their users". The administration has also vowed to improve security measures by increasing Internet supervision and strengthening law enforcement. For instance, citizens were encouraged by the administration to report any information present online that is 'harmful.' It is clear that the crackdown by the CAC is likely to affect indigenous companies as much as foreign ones.[38]

Hacking and Other Cyber attacks
A notable aspect of cyber attacks that is relevant to this paper is espionage efforts by Country A aimed at gaining entry into the cyber

systems of Country B to monitor activities and extract information using systems located in Country C. In this context, Brookings' report on cyber security and US-China relations identifies three features of capturing and utilising online systems and computers:

1. There are no geographical limits: this would permit a malevolent actor in Country A to compromise computers in Country B to launch an attack on systems in Country C.
2. The owner of the captured computer is unaware of the system being used for malevolent purposes.
3. Finally, when malevolent activity is perpetrated, analysis may help identify the computer being used to launch the attack, but it is difficult to determine by whom the attack has been launched.[39]

This complex web of ambiguity results in greater problems. Spectators are inclined to believe that the Chinese government is behind the malicious activities launched by computers in China, but also acknowledge that it is possible that the actors in this case might only be using Chinese computers as part of their activities. This argument allows Chinese actors engaging in such activity to deny responsibility and claim that the activities were perpetrated by someone who is located elsewhere but is looking to take advantage of the suspicions directed towards China.[40]

Cyber attacks constitute a large number of offences and activities that range from vandalism or mischief to causing strategic harm to a country's capabilities. A culmination of malevolent technology and aggressive political strategy may lead to what some scholars call "cyber warfare".[41]

Other Modes of Information Control: Curbing Academic Freedom

In a recent move in August 2017, the Chinese government demanded that nearly 300 articles from *China Quarterly* (a reputed news journal on contemporary China studies in the world) be taken down.[42] Cambridge University Press (CUP) blocked readers in China from accessing articles that were based on certain topics, including the Tiananmen Square protests, Tibet, the Cultural Revolution, democracy and human rights.[43] Offering an explanation for the move, an editorial piece in the *Global Times* described the move as a "matter of principle". The piece further demanded conformity to Chinese laws from the "West", so that they could continue to engage in business with the Chinese market. It is also termed academic freedom a "Western concept".[44]

Spectators and critics have responded harshly to this crackdown on intellectual freedom. Yang Guobin, a member of *China Quarterly*'s editorial team, took to Weibo to express his thoughts, wherein he questioned the Chinese government's apparent attempt to curb contemporary Chinese studies.[45]

Jonathan Sullivan, Director of the China Policy Institute, declared the politicisation of academic research "anathema" and further went on to locate the ban within the context of a larger trend of increasing control over various realms of society.[46] Following similar responses from several quarters, the CUP reinstated the blocked articles in the Chinese mainland.[47]

The challenge of censorship faced by publishers, domestic and international alike, must be taken seriously. The freedom of academicians and intellectuals has been severely undermined; the repercussions of China's censorship policies are creating ripples in the international Chinese academic network as well. This poses a threat to the Chinese academic community and restricts the production of critical and insightful work on China. Such policies are also detrimental to China's quest to improve inter-connectedness and further its goals of expanding into a global market. Another point of importance is the potential breach of human rights regulations that could unfold in the days to come. In the meantime, spectators behold the unravelling of Chinese policy with both anxiety and anticipation.

China and Other International Organisations on the Topic of Cyber Space

China's call for cyber sovereignty does not prevent bodies such as the United Nations and the World Trade Organisation from acting on issues of concern in the cyber realm. In his speech at the World Internet

Conference, 2015, President Xi stated that "the rule enshrined in the charter of the United Nations is one of the basic rules in contemporary international relations".[48]

China has been working closely with the United Nations in the realm of matters concerning cyber space. The Shanghai Cooperation Organisation (SCO), (of which China, Russia, Uzbekistan, Tajikistan, Kyrgyzstan and Kazakhstan are part) is an organisation that has been involved in the development of guidelines in cyber space. In 2001, the SCO adopted a "Convention on Combating Terrorism, Separatism and Extremism" which came into force in 2003. An agreement on "Cooperation in the Field of Information Security" was made in 2008.[49]

Since the beginning of the new millennium, China and Russia have co-sponsored and pushed for a number of reforms in cyber space, most of which have not been met with approval due to contesting views with the 'West'. While the US seeks to limit cyber attacks and espionage, China looks towards addressing "broader rules" that could contain a state's ability to use cyber space for malicious purposes. In 2011, China, Russia, Tajikistan and Uzbekistan drafted an International Code of Conduct (CoC) for information security and requested the United Nations Secretary General to distribute it as a formal document at the 66th session of General Assembly.[50]

According to the CoC, signatory countries would not be allowed to use "ICTs, including networks to carry out hostile activities or acts of aggression and pose threats to international peace and security. Not to proliferate information weapons and related technologies."[51] The draft also sought to legalise state control of the Internet, a stance that the United States and other nations from the West did not support. In addition to this, the draft also called for a multilateral method of managing the Internet. The draft called for restricting "dissemination of information which incites terrorism, secessionism, extremism or undermines other countries' political, economic and social stability, as well as their spiritual and cultural environment". Many countries from the West perceived this as a way of restricting freedom of expression. Predictably, the draft received little support from countries in the West.[52]

China continues to push for reforms in the existing global Internet. A recent report released in March 2017 by the Ministry of Foreign Affairs and the Cyber Space Administration of China, called "International Strategy of Cooperation on the Cyber Space", has reiterated China's firm resolve to ensure that no one nation can control cyber space. As also mentioned by President Xi at the World Internet Conference, the document reinforces the thought that "countries should reject the Cold War mentality, zero-sum game and double standards, uphold peace through cooperation and seek one's own security through common security on the basis of full respect for other countries' security."[53, 54] The document, however, discourages the use of ICT to interfere in other countries' affairs. It also calls for reforms in the UN's role in managing Internet governance: it advocates the "institutional reform of the UN Internet Governance Forum to enable it to play a greater role in Internet governance, strengthen its decision-making capacity, secure steady funding, and introduce open and transparent procedures in its members' election and report submission".[55] Finally, China has shown its support for the reform of ICANN to make it fully independent and transparent.

India and Cyber Sovereignty: Problems and Prospects
A body of significance that must be considered in the context of India and cyber space governance is BRICS (a grouping consisting of Brazil, Russia, India, China and South Africa). The next BRICS Summit is expected to convene in September 2017 in Xiamen. During the summit, India, Brazil and South Africa (IBSA) will have the option of voicing their thoughts on the Sino-Russian agenda to implement state control of cyber space. All the nations involved in the decision-making process are large stakeholders in the modern day Internet governance. Besides having essayed determining roles in the transfer of the control of IANA functions in 2016, the BRICS nations also boast of large Internet penetration rates; they play a decisive role in cyber space governance. Member nations of BRICS, including India, face the challenging task of balancing national security and economic necessity.[56]

Experts at the Observer Research Foundation (ORF) believe that India is unlikely to side with China on the agreement that would bind members into a multilateral treaty on cyber sovereignty. According to one expert, India already endorses the freedom of each country to perform sovereign functions.[57] India, in the BRICS Summit at Goa in 2016, had already signed a Memorandum of Understanding with Russia that safeguards critical infrastructure and prevents cyber crime. In addition to this, there are practical problems that could upset the precarious Indo-Sino ties. Further, India would not be well-equipped to deal with cyber sovereignty in a situation where a large number of Indian servers are located abroad. India, unlike China, does not follow data localisation policies and does not wield much control over its networks and servers.[58]

Returning to the discussion on BRICS, member nations would do well to arrive at the golden mean in Internet governance norms to combat the escalating concerns in cyber space. Cyber security experts recommend that all members assert their authority while negotiating ICT norms. The challenge, however, is to accomplish the same without straying from the democratic principles of Internet governance. It is to be seen how the member countries of BRICS respond to the Chinese call for cyber sovereignty.[59]

Apple in China: A Brief Case Study on How the American MNC Operates in China

According to a study published in the *Harvard Business Review*, China is Apple's fastest growing market. Apple officially opened its stores to the Chinese public in 2008, prior to which Apple products were sold in the Chinese grey market.[60] Since their entry into the Chinese market several years ago, iPhones have lured customers. This trend propelled Apple to the top of the Chinese smartphone market in December 2014. In March 2015, Apple's performance and revenue in Greater China overtook that in Europe, making it Apple's second-biggest market after the US.[61]

Apple is an American multinational company whose presence in China is of interest for a number of reasons. Among them is that fact that Apple has agreed to the cyber space rules laid down by the Chinese administration. Following a meeting between Apple CEO Tim Cook and former Chinese cyber space official Lu Wei in January 2015, the *People's Daily*, known to be the Chinese government's mouthpiece, tweeted: "Apple has agreed to accept China's security checks, 1st foreign firm to agree to rules of Cyber space Admin of China"[62]

Fig 2: Former Chinese Cyber Space Official and Current Head of the Propaganda Department of the CCP, Lu Wei

Source: Wikimedia Commons (www.https://upload.wikimedia.org/wikipedia/commons/4/4e/Lu_Wei_2015.jpg)

Apple's rise as one of China's more popular foreign electronics companies has not been without roadblocks. Apple has made more compromises in the Chinese market than it has made on its own turf. The company has battled a national security backlash and has censored apps that did not meet with approval from the Chinese authorities. Local user data has been moved into servers operated by China Telecom, which is state owned. The company also submits to state audits by Chinese authorities. Apple has not shown such compliance even in the face of a Federal Bureau of Investigation (FBI) order to decrypt the phone of a suspected hit man. In Apple's defence, spokespersons have stated that consenting to the FBI's demands may set a precedent for China to demand the same.[63]

Apple was also caught in the eye of the storm in 2013, when the Edward Snowden – National Security Agency (NSA) leak came to light. Questions were raised by Chinese state-run media about Apple's location-tracking feature. In what was a strong show of Chinese techno-nationalism, Party cadres and other officials were discouraged from using Apple devices. Some spectators believe this to be a move in response to the threat of likely social unrest. In the thick of this furore, Apple announced its decision to migrate and shift its data to China-based servers. However, Apple also added that all the data was encrypted and was inaccessible to servers at China Telecom. Leading iPhone security experts are still sceptical of Chinese servers and contest that the data remains susceptible to confiscation or "cryptanalysis".[64]

Most of the hardware that has been hacked at Apple earlier has come from China. Experts believe that the relationship formed between Apple and China puts the US at considerable risk.[65] China has also made a market of counterfeit Apple products that were produced following the success of the iPhone: "Apple's popularity in China led to considerable counterfeiting or copying of their prototypes, products, knowhow, trade secrets, service model, and store concepts."[66]

It is crucial to understand why Apple places China in a position of importance. A likely reason for this could be that China is home to Apple's manufacturing services. Shutting down the manufacturing vendor Hon Hai (also called the Foxconn Technology Group) could deliver a harsh blow to Apple in a matter of days. Although India, Taiwan, Thailand, Japan and South Korea are leading alternatives for setting up manufacturing units, none of them show the potential of coming up to speed over the next five years.[67]

Recently, in July 2017, Apple removed VPN services from its app-store. VPNs or Virtual Private Networks allow users to circumvent censored websites. Users can access blocked networks by hiding their Internet Protocol (IP) addresses. Apple has stated that the removal of the VPNs was required as they did not comply with the existing regulations (in January 2017, China's Ministry of Industry and Information Technology announced that all developers offering VPN services must obtain authorisation from the government.)[68]

Some of the VPN companies affected by this decision have stated that Apple has "sided with censorship" by removing VPN apps. Golden

Frog, a VPN company, expressed the need for Apple to place human rights over profit-making, since international bodies, including the UN, have deemed the Internet a basic human right.[69]

While Apple continues to cooperate with China's state security measures, Tim Cook has made his word on encryption final. Should China express its desire to further push Apple into revealing source-codes and installing backdoors as part of its drive to ensure national security, Apple may have to look for a new manufacturing destination.

What Lies Ahead: An Assessment of the Impact of Cyber Sovereignty
Cyber sovereignty has multiple implications on various levels for China. This section will attempt to examine the impact of cyber sovereignty on some spheres of significance.

Digital Silk Road: A Marriage of Economy with Technology
China's most recent initiative to project itself as the flag bearer of globalisation is the One Belt One Road (OBOR) strategy. The two major segments of this initiative that received attention were the Silk Road Economic Belt (which runs through Central Asia to Europe) and 21st Century Maritime Silk Road (which goes through Southeast Asia, Africa and Europe).[70] The massive infrastructure project also has a third, lesser-known component pertaining to cyber space: the Digital Silk Road initiative.

There are several key aspects of the Digital Silk Road plan or the 'Information Silk Road'. While the development of this initiative is in the early stages, this section shall attempt to weigh the merits and demerits of the Digital Silk Road in the context of cyber sovereignty. China's new digital segment aims to enhance digital connectivity and build and maintain seamless data connections. However, communication networks built by China may fall prey to network fractures, especially if the route travels through the US and Europe, where countries will look to shield their data due to surveillance fears.[71] This would render a large segment of the network redundant. Cyber sovereignty, here, allows for countries to manage their data security according to national security requirements, and cannot be contested.

The OBOR-Digital Silk Road initiative also gives China the opportunity to encourage use of the BeiDou satellite network, a rival network to the Global Positioning System (GPS) that is expected to deliver global coverage by 2020. Limited use of the BeiDou network is already underway in Karachi, Pakistan.[72] The development of BeiDou as a fully-fledged network has implications for the US as the People's Liberation Army (PLA) is expected to step up its weapons and tracking abilities. According to the report released by the US-China Economic and Security Review Commission in January 2017, the concern is that "BeiDou could pose a security risk by allowing China's government to track users of the system by deploying malware transmitted through either its navigation signal or messaging function (via a satellite communication channel), once the technology is in widespread use."[73] This once again indicates that China may not be able to adhere to the cyber sovereignty that it so desires other countries to adopt.

Two of China's e-commerce giants — Alibaba and JD.com — have already pledged their participation and support for the OBOR initiative. Both companies see the countries lining the OBOR trail as important regions for trade and expansion.[74] While the Chinese companies' ambitions to expand global trade dovetails with the OBOR's plans to explore new trade routes, they are likely to face competition from local firms, infrastructure constraints and regulatory restrictions. Commentators from the Council on Foreign Relations argue that there are many obstacles for these companies to tackle before they can enjoy commercial success. They also conclude, "Surveying the digital landscape under the auspices of One Belt, One Road, many projects still appear linked by political rhetoric rather than a coherent strategy."[75] They believe that if these challenges can be surpassed, the Digital Silk Road has great potential in linking other countries to Chinese networks and cap the influence of the US in this realm. Some commentators also believe that China would do well to reduce the stigma of cyber espionage to catalyse its ambitions of emerging a leader in the global market and in the US.

Cyber Security Challenges to Military Security

China's use of cyber technology and espionage methods has escalated the dispute concerning a group of 14 islands in the South China Sea. These islands, called the Spratly Islands, are a region of economic and strategic importance, located in the middle of several important trade routes. Apart from being home to fishing grounds, the possibility of their containing natural resources makes them extremely valuable. China, Vietnam and the Philippines have made claims to these islands as their own. China has recently adopted a more aggressive tone in its strategy to claim these islands — by building artificial islands as well as by carrying out military operations there.[76]

Fig 3: Map of the Spratly and Paracel Islands

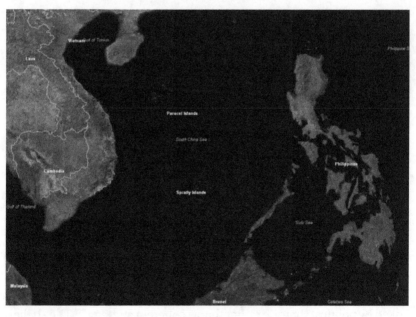

Source: Wikimedia Commons (www.https://upload.wikimedia.org/wikipedia/
commons/thumb/4/4a/Spratly_%26_Paracel_Islands.png/1024px-
Spratly_%26_Paracel_Islands.png)

After an international court ruled against China in this case, China launched a series of DDoS attacks on 68 Philippine government websites in July 2016. Following this, Vietnam's national airline and major airports were targeted in a series of attacks by a Chinese hacking group, 1937CN.[77] China has been assertively claiming the islands for a many years now. Also threatened by these attacks are the US military systems in the South China Sea. China has shown an inclination towards employing cyber and electronics attacks to help take control of American military drones. In another instance, China also attempted to interfere with the American drones by showing willingness to use 'GPS jamming' to prevent the US from organising surveillance missions in the Spratly Islands. The jamming is predicted to be the biggest threat to the American drone system.[78]In response to this, the US released a Department of Defence Cyber Strategy (also mentioned under the 'Intellectual Property Rights' section of this paper), outlining its new plan to include cyber strategy in military planning. The report also calls for strengthening of military defence to be able to avoid attacks on military weaponry and theft of military technology.[79]

Owing to a dispute with China over the Diaoyu Islands, the Japanese were rendered victims of a series of cyber attacks in 2012. The Japanese government reported that 11 out of 19 websites which include those of the Defence Ministry and Internal Affairs and Communications Ministry were struck by DDoS attacks. The site of the Tokyo Institute of Technology was defaced by the image of the Chinese flag. In addition to this, details of over 100 staff members of the institute were leaked. The islands in question have been claimed by both China and Taiwan since the 1960s and are speculated to be a source of valuable oil deposits.[80]

On the topic of reforms, the military reforms introduced by President Xi have not fallen behind on including components of cyber space strategy within their framework. A reform introduced towards the end of 2015 includes 'cyber space and electronic warfare operations' as part of the PLA's Strategic Support Force's portfolio.[81]China's stance on the inclusion of military strategy in the cyber realm (and vice-versa) however, reads contrary to this. The *International Strategy of Co-operation on Cyber Space* declares:

The tendency of militarization and deterrence buildup in cyber space is not conducive to international security and strategic mutual trust. China encourages all parties to commit to peaceful settlement of disputes, non-use or threat of force and other basic norms in international relations and put in place consultation and mediation mechanisms to forestall and avoid conflict, so that cyber space will not become a new battlefield.[82]

Cyber attacks have, thus, made their way into traditional forms of combat and diplomacy. It remains to be seen how China can set an example for cyber sovereignty while reportedly engaging in cyber attacks of considerable magnitude.

Conclusion: Making Cyber Space More Conducive to Progress
Beijing continues to make attempts to reduce its dependence on foreign technology by using legal administrative practices to further its goal of cyber sovereignty. However, as outlined in the paper, some demands made by China have led to debates surrounding intellectual property theft, source-code declaration requirements and prevention of cross-border flow of data. These policies require rethinking before China can proceed to make a call for cyber sovereignty.

Some of the data presented above, supplemented by a deeper reading of the Chinese discourse on cyber sovereignty, reveal that Chinese notions and formulations on the topic are yet to take definite shape. Implementation of cyber sovereignty poses far more challenges and requires a larger consensus than that which exists. This is a shortcoming in the formulation of the Chinese foreign policy itself, wherein political thoughts lack clarity when proposed and discussed. Providing clarity and transparency about cyber sovereignty in the domestic realm will help reduce the inconsistency and bridge the gap between ideas and action at the international level.[83]

China shares common interests with a number of foreign markets, including the US. While it is indisputable that they harbour ideological differences, it is to be seen how China tackles differences and prevents these differences from derailing its relationship with these countries.

On the subject of US-China relations, the topic of cyber space and cyber security in the Chinese context is yet to take a position of importance under the leadership of President Donald Trump. Meetings between former US President Barack Obama and President Xi had proved fruitful in promoting cyber diplomacy. Chinese cyber attacks were reported to have reduced in number following talks between the two leaders. Spectators are keen to observe whether these issues will be given the same priority during President Trump's tenure and if his team can successfully tackle the challenges presented by the Chinese cyber activity.[84]

Nevertheless, the US-China relationship in cyber space requires further examination. According to experts, there is every possibility of a crisis breaking out. For instance, the forces of both the US and People's Republic of China (PRC) are deployed in the South China Sea. In this context, a cyber attack on either side could cause the situation to spiral out of control.[85] Hackers further deteriorate the situation by negating the possibility of negotiations between the two sides, as neither side can fully understand the intent and origin of an attack. This problem is also reflected in the case of non-state actors or 'patriotic hackers', who make it difficult for policy-makers to differentiate between an official attack and an independent one. Cooperation between countries assumes greater significance in the face of increasingly sophisticated technology and well-planned cyber attacks by third parties.

Fig 4: President Xi with President Trump, April 2017

Source: Wikimedia Commons (https://upload.wikimedia.org/wikipedia/commons/
thumb/0/09/President_Trump_with_President_Xi%2C_April_2017.jpg/1024px-
President_Trump_with_President_Xi%2C_April_2017.jpg)

Recommendations for a 'Beijing-Washington' hotline have previously been made to help de-escalate a situation in case of emergencies in cyber space. Some experts have referred to this provision as the 'cyber hotline', while others call it the 'red phone'.[86, 87]

On the topic of Internet companies, China is home to four of the top ten Internet companies in the world.[88] If these companies are to expand globally, China must extend its support and respect the cyber sovereignty of other countries. Cyber security agreements must be followed-up and talks on these matters must continue even during times of duress and tension. Trust can only be created and sustained through action. As suggested by some experts, with regard to discussion on cyber space, "dialogue must be formalised, routinised and insulated from political point scoring".[89] China's aims to reinforce cyber sovereignty, however, will not remain unchallenged. In a world that has collectively learnt to value and respect information sharing and free flow of data, the curbing of such basic rights is expected to be met with dissent. The future of Chinese cyber space holds significant opportunities in the digital, military and economic spheres. These opportunities are within arm's reach for China if it can reconcile its goals of claiming global power and safeguarding its 'national security'. Nevertheless, the steady rise of the Sinosphere is worth following closely in 2017 and in the years to come.

Notes

1. Centre for Strategic and International Studies, "How Web-Connected is China?" 2016-2017. Accessed on June 23, 2017, http://chinapower.csis.
2. "The 2nd WIC Organizing Committee Proposes the Wuzhen Initiative," World Internet Conference, Wuzhen Summit, December 18, 2015. Accessed on June 23, 2017, www.wuzhenwic.org/2015-12/18/c_48241.htm.
3. "Why Does Cyber Sovereignty Matter?" *China Daily*, December 16, 2015. Accessed on June 27, www.chinadaily.com/cn/business/tech/2015-12/16/content_22728202.htm, 2017.
4. Jinghan Zeng, Yaru Chen, and Tim Stevens, *China's Solution to Global Cyber Governance: Unpacking the Domestic Discourse of "Internet Sovereignty* (Wiley, 2017).
5. "Stewardship of IANA Functions Transitions to Global Internet Community as Contract with US Government Ends," *ICANN*, October 1, 2016. Accessed on June 27, 2017, https://www.icann.org/news/announcement-2016-10-01-en.
6. Ibid.
7. Steve Crocker, "Cheers to the Multistakeholder Community," *ICANN*, September 30, 2016. Accessed on June 27, 2017, https://www.icann.org/news/blogs/cheers-to-the-multistakeholder-community.
8. "Why Does Cyber Sovereignty Matter?" *China Daily*, December 16, 2015. Accessed on June 27, 2017, www.chinadaily.com/cn/business/tech/2015-12/16/content_22728202.htm.
9. n.2.
10. William H. Dutton, "Multistakeholder Internet Governance?" *World Development Report 2016*, pp.1-33.
11. Ibid.
12. n.2.
13. Jon R. Lindsay, "The Impact of China on Cybersecurity," *International Security*, 2015, pp.14-15.
14. "China Headlines: Xi Slams 'Double Standards,' Advocates Shared Future in Cyber Space," *Xinhuanet*, December 16, 2015. Accessed July 1, 2017, news.xinhuanet.com/english/indepth/2015-12/16/c_134924012.htm.

15. Kenneth Lieberthal and Peter W. Singer, *Cybersecurity and US-China Relations* (Brookings, 2012).

16. Ibid.

17. Ibid.

18. Lindsay, n.13.

19. Josh Rogin, "The Top 10 Chinese Cyber Attacks (That We Know Of)." *Foreign Policy,* January 22, 2010. Accessed on July 1, 2017, http://foreignpolicy.com/2010/01/22/the-top-10-chinese-cyber attacks-that-we-know-of/

20. Kate Conger, "China's New Cyber Security Law is Bad News for Business," *TechCrunch,* November 6, 2016. Accessed on July 1, 2017, https://techcrunch.com/2016/11/06/chinas-new-cybersecurity-law-is-bad-news-for-business.

21. Adam Segal, *China, Encryption Policy, and International Influence* (Stanford: Hoover Institution, Stanford University, 2016).

22. Ibid.

23. Ibid.

24. Ibid.

25. Cory Bennet, "China Wants Cyber Sovereignty in Latest National Security Law," *The Hill,* August 5, 2015. Accessed on July 1, 2017, thehill.com/policy/cybersecurity/241420-china-wants-cyber sovereignty-in-the-latest-national-security-law.

26. Segal, n.21.

27. William New, "After 15 Years in WTO, China Still Weak On Many IP Rights Rules, US Says," *Intellectual Property Watch,* January 1, 2017. Accessed July 1, 2017, https://www.ip-watch.org/2017/01/10/15-years-wto-china-still-weak-many-ip-rights-rules-us-says/.

28. United States Trade Representative, *2016 Report to Congress on China's WTO Compliance,* 2017.

29. New, n.27

30. n.28.

31. The Department of Defence, United States of America, *The DoD Cyber Strategy* (Washington, DC: The Department of Defence, 2015).

32. Jack Perkowski, "Protecting Intellectual Property Rights in China," *Forbes,* April 18, 2012. Accessed on July 1, 2017, https://forbes.com/sites/jackperkowski/2012/04/18/protecting-intellectual-property-rights-in-china/#7dc0e3353458.

33. KPMG, *Overview of China's Cybersecurity Law* (KPMG, 2017).

34. Samm Sacks, "China's Cybersecurity Law Takes Effect: What to Expect." *Lawfare,* June 1, 2017. Accessed on July 1, 2017, https://www.lawfareblog.com/chinas-cybersecurity-law-takes-effect-what-expect.

35. "CAC Releases Cross-Border Data Transfer Security Assessment Measures," *United States Information Technology Office.* Accessed on July 1, 2017, http://www.usito.org/news/cac-releases-cross-border-data-transfer-security-assessment-measures.

36. Sacks, n.34.

37. Ibid.

38. Charlotte Gao, "China Accuses Its Top 3 Internet Giants of Potentially Violating Cybersecurity Law," *The Diplomat,* August 12, 2017. Accessed on August 15, 2017, ://thediplomat.com/2017/08/china-accuses-its-top-3-internet-giants-of-potentially-violating-cybersecurity-law/?utm_content=buffer05d11&utm_medium=social&utm_source=twitter.com&utm_campaign=buffer.

39. Lieberthal, and Singer, n.15.

40. Ibid.

41. Lindsay, n.13.

42. Sonika Gupta, "Staring Down Censorship," *The Hindu,* September 6, 2017. Accessed on September 8, 2017, http://www.thehindu.com/opinion/op-ed/staring-down-censorship/article19626142.ece.

43. Richard Adams, "Cambridge University Press Blocks Readers in China From Articles," *The Guardian,* August 17, 2017. Accessed on September 8, 2017, https://www.theguardian.com/education/2017/aug/18/cambridge-university-press-blocks-readers-china-quarterly.

44. Ibid.

45. Echo Huang and Isabella Stenger, "Forced to Comply or Shut Down, Cambridge University Press's China Quarterly removes 300 Articles in China," *Quartz,* August 18, 2017. Accessed on September 8, 2017, https://qz.com/1056938/cambridge-university-press-china-quarterly-complies-with-censorship-removes-300-articles-on-topics-like-tiananmen-and-tibet-in-china/.

46. Jonathan Sullivan, "Censorship and China Studies," *China Policy Institute: Analysis,* August 19, 2017. Accessed on September 8, 2017, https://cpianalysis.org/2017/08/19/censorship-and-china-studies/.

47. Ibid.

48. "'President Xi Jinping Delivers a Keynote Speech at 2015 World Internet Conference," China Global Television Network, December 15, 2015.

49. Stein Schjolberg, "A Geneva Declaration for Cyber Space," 2016.

50. "The UN and Cyber Space Governance," Observer Research Foundation, February 1, 2014. Accessed on July 1, 2017, www.orfonline.org/article/the-un-and-cyber space-governance/.

51. Ibid.

52. Ibid.

53. Simon Sharwood, "China Proposes New World Order for Cyber Space Regulation," *The Register,* March 2, 2017. Accessed on July 1, 2017, https://www.theregister.co.uk/2017/03/02/china_international_strategy_of_cooperation_on_cyber space/.

54. "Full Text: International Strategy of Cooperation on Cyber Space," *Xinhuanet,* March 1, 2017. Accessed on July 1, 2017, news.xinhuanet.com/english/china/2017-03/01/c_136094371_2.htm.

55. Ibid.

56. Madhulika Srikumar, "Should BRICS Rally Around China's Call for Cyber Sovereignty?" Observer Research Foundation, June 2, 2017. Accessed on July 1, 2017, http://www.orfonline.org/expert-speaks/should-brics-rally-around-china-call-for-cyber sovereignty/.

57. "India Not Eager to Hop on to China's Cyber Sovereignty Bandwagon," *Sputnik News,* 2017. Accessed on August 15, 2017, https://sptnkne.ws/fjBS.

58. Ibid.

59. Srikumar, n.56.

60. Mary B Teagarden, "Apple in China," *Harvard Business Review,* 2016.

61. "Apple in China," IBS Centre for Management Studies, 2015.

62. Retrieved from https://twitter.com/PDChina/status/558353534958469123/photo/1?ref_src=twsrc%5Etfw&ref_url=https%3A%2F%2Ftechcrunch.com%2F2016%2F04%2F19%2Fapples-head-of-legal-says-it-refused-chinas-request-for-its-source-code%2F (Twitter update by *People's Daily,* China on January 22, 2015).

63. David Pierson, "While It Defies US Government, Apple Abides by China's Orders - And Reaps Big Rewards," *Los Angeles Times,* February 26, 2016. Accessed on July 1, 2017, www.latimes.com/business/technology/la-fi-apple-china-20160226-story.html

64. Ibid.

65. Ibid.

66. Teagarden, n.60.

67. Robin Harris, "Apple's Biggest China Problem," *Storage Bits,* May 2, 2016. Accessed on July 1, 2017, www.zdnet.com/article/apples-biggest-china-problem/.

68. "Apple 'Pulls 60 VPNs from China App Store'," BBC News, July 31, 2017. Accessed on August 8, 2017, http://www.bbc.com/news/technology-40772375.

69. Ibid.

70. Rachel Brown, "Beijing's Silk Road Goes Digital," Council on Foreign Relations, June 6, 2017. Accessed on July 1, 2017, https://www.cfr.org/blog-post/beijings-silk-road-goes-digital.

71. Nadege Rolland, "A Fiber-Optic Silk Road," *The Diplomat,* April 2, 2015. Accessed on July 1, 2017, thediplomat.com/2015/04/a-fiber-optic-silk-road/.

72. Jonathan Moss, Lipton James and Sophie Hoffman, "The South China Sea: The Spratly Islands Dispute," The Centre of Expertise on Asia, July 18, 2016. Accessed on July 1, 2017, asiahouse.org/the-south-china-sea-the-spratly-islands-dispute/

73. Jordon Wilson, *China's Alternative to GPS and its Implications for the United States,* US-China Economic and Security Review Commission, 2017.

74. Brown, n.70.

75. Ibid.

76. Moss, et. al., n.72.

77. Paul Martini, "Cybersecurity is Threatening America's Military Supremacy,"

TechCrunch, September 21, 2016. Accessed on July 1, 2017, https://techcrunch. com/2016/09/21/cybersecurity-is-threatening-americas-military-supremacy/.

78. Ibid.

79. n.31.

80. Phil Muncaster, "Chinese Hacktivists Launch Cyber Attack on Japan," *The Register,* September 21, 2012. Accessed on July 1, 2017, https://www.theregister. co.uk/2012/09/21/japan_china_attack_sites_senkaku/.

81. "China Takes Bold Steps Toward Military Reform," *Stratfor Worldview,* January 11, 2016. Accessed on July 1, 2017, https://worldview.stratfor.com/analysis/ china-takes-bold-steps-toward-military-reform.

82. n.54.

83. Zeng, n.4.

84. Jesse Heatley, "Cybersecurity Must Top Agenda as Trump Hosts Xi," *The Diplomat,* April 5, 2017. Accessed on July 1, 2017, http://thediplomat. com/2017/04/cybersecurity-must-top-agenda-as-trump-hosts-xi/.

85. Adam Segal and Tang Lan, "Can the United States and China De-Conflict in Cyber Space?" *Texas National Security Network,* April 27, 2016. Accessed July 1, 2017, https://warontherocks.com/2016/04/can-united-states-and-china-de-conflict-in-cyber space/.

86. Adam Segal, "US-China Cyber Hotline?" *The Diplomat,* December 1, 2011. Accessed on July 1, 2017, http://thediplomat.com/2011/12/us-china-cyber-hotline/.

87. Clay Dillow, "China Daily: There Should Be a Beijing-Washington Hotline to Avoid Cyber-Misunderstandings," *Popular Science,* December 2, 2011. Accessed on July 1, 2017, http://www.popsci.com/technology/article/2011-12/china-daily-us-and-china-need-beijing.

88. Lu Wei, "Cyber Sovereignty Must Rule Global Internet," *Huffpost.* Accessed on July 1, 2017, www.huufingtonpost.com/lu-wei/china-cyber sovereignty_b_5324060.html.

89. Segal and Lan, n.85.